PATRICK H. PERRINE

Unicorn Manifesto

The Ascent of an Entrepreneur from Startup to Acquisition

DEDICATION

To you, standing at the brink of boundless possibilities, This book is your compass, dedicated to the fiery passion and courage within you. May "Unicorn Manifesto" be the whisper of wisdom from trailblazers past, guiding every step of your journey. Every legend starts with a leap. With this guide, leap fearlessly and reach for the stars.

Warmly,
Patrick

"Your work is going to fill a large part of your life, and the only way to be truly satisfied is to do what you believe is great work. And the only way to do great work is to love what you do."

— STEVE JOBS

Contents

Preface

In a world bursting with untapped potential and visionary ideas, it's the entrepreneurs who dare to dream—and do—who truly stand out. If you're holding 'Unicorn Manifesto: The Ascent of an Entrepreneur from Startup to Acquisition,' you're not just holding a book. You're clutching the compass that will guide you through the tempestuous yet exhilarating journey of entrepreneurship, inspired directly by my book 'Unicorn Rising.'

This volume serves as your practical companion to 'Unicorn Rising,' specifically designed to deepen your understanding and application of the principles laid out in Step 1: 'Odyssey of Opportunity: An Entrepreneur's Voyage from Ideation to Acquisition.' As the first of a ten-volume series, 'Unicorn Manifesto' is both a beacon and a toolkit, offering a structured, step-by-step guide to transforming your entrepreneurial dreams into reality.

Crafted from the wisdom gleaned through countless hours of research, firsthand entrepreneurial success stories, and the cumulative knowledge of the world's leading business minds, this series is tailored for you—the innovator, the disruptor, the dreamer.

As 'Unicorn Manifesto' navigates the journey from the initial spark of an idea to the strategic maneuvers leading to a successful acquisition, it is your North Star in the entrepreneurial cosmos. It lights the path to innovation, resilience, and growth, guiding you through each step with clarity and purpose.

However, this path is not without its trials. The journey of an entrepreneur is marked by challenges, uncertainties, and moments of doubt. Yet, it is through these very challenges that the essence of a unicorn is forged—transforming obstacles into opportunities for unparalleled success.

As you embark on this reading journey, you're also embarking on a personal voyage of discovery and transformation. 'Unicorn Manifesto' is not just a book; it's your entry into an odyssey of personal and professional growth—a journey that mirrors the entrepreneurial spirit of 'Unicorn Rising' and extends its narrative into actionable insights and strategies for your success.

Are you ready to begin this extraordinary adventure? With 'Unicorn Manifesto' in hand, the path to becoming a unicorn in a world of horses is not just a possibility—it's your destiny.

Be A Unicorn: The New Entrepreneur's Ultimate Guide To Success

Dream It, Build It:
An Aspirational Odyssey Through
Entrepreneurship in Ten Inspiring Volumes.

Volume One

UNICORN MANIFESTO
The Ascent of an Entrepreneur from Startup to Acquisition

1

Starting Right: Laying the Groundwork for Your Entrepreneurial Dream

"The best way to predict the future is to create it."
— Peter Drucker

Welcome to the first volume of "Be A Unicorn: The New Entrepreneur's Ultimate Guide to Success." Here, we prioritize action, tangible results, and equipping you to turn your idea into a thriving enterprise. I'm Patrick H. Perrine, and after two decades of experience in startup creation, development, and scaling, my goal is to arm you with the insights needed to shape your unique entrepreneurial journey.

Anecdote Corner: Let me share a brief story. During the early days of my second startup, we were struggling to get user engagement. Instead of dwelling on potential product issues, we organized a face-to-face feedback session with some of our users. It was during this session that we realized a small UI issue was causing a major disruption. It wasn't a product flaw; it was a design oversight! This incident reinforced the idea that sometimes, solutions lie outside the box, and a direct approach can save time and resources.

Why This Guide? This isn't just another book that pontificates on entrepreneurship; it's your precise roadmap. Catering to both seasoned pros and newcomers, the content here delivers real-world strategies, actionable methods, and advice to navigate the entire startup journey. Real-life cases and testimonies threaded throughout these chapters add depth to the theories presented.

The Entrepreneurial Tenets: Every entrepreneur's path is unique, but some tenets and practices are time-tested. We'll decode these, translating the occasionally nebulous startup process into clear, actionable steps. You'll also find practical checklists at the end of each chapter, ensuring you stay on track.

Core Values: Success hinges on determination, willingness for calculated risk, adaptability, and an insatiable thirst for knowledge. Through interviews and insights from industry veterans, we'll dissect how these values played pivotal roles in their success stories. You'll encounter challenges, but it's your unwavering commitment to these values that will guide you towards unforeseen opportunities.

The Journey Ahead: In upcoming chapters, we'll delve into pivotal stages of the entrepreneurial process, from ideation and MVP creation to financing, scaling, and the subtleties of exits and acquisitions. Alongside these technical aspects, we'll spotlight the personal growth accompanying each phase.

No Magic Bullet: It's crucial to understand that this guide isn't a panacea. The entrepreneurial landscape is ever-changing, each venture presenting its unique challenges. Yet, insights from seasoned entrepreneurs, combined with reflection exercises and mindset tools, can significantly tilt the odds in your favor.

Redefining 'Unicorn': Today, 'unicorn' is synonymous with startups valued over $1 billion. However, it's not just about high valuations. Authentic unicorns seamlessly blend value with sustainable growth and real profitability. This guide highlights the intrinsic qualities genuine unicorns possess, looking beyond mere billion-dollar tags to the core ingredients of prolonged success. Through case studies, we'll uncover the strategies behind several "unicorn" successes and failures, shedding light on the nuances of each journey.

The True Essence of Entrepreneurship: Entrepreneurship is more than chasing accolades. It's an odyssey of passion, vision, and innovation. It's about crafting an endeavor that excels not just in valuation but in value offered. Throughout this guide, we'll punctuate our discussions with inspiring stories from the trenches, painting a holistic view of the entrepreneurial world.

Ready for Transformation? Are you set to embark on this transformative journey? As we delve deeper, our first stop is the foundational phase of ideation and validation, spotlighting the art of cultivating and evaluating business ideas and emphasizing the importance of exhaustive market research.

Join us in charting your unique entrepreneurial story. Together, we'll traverse the multifaceted terrain of startups, fortifying each phase with actionable insights, expert testimonies, and hands-on exercises to cement your learning.

2

Igniting the Flame: Ideation and Validation

"The value of an idea lies in the using of it."
— Thomas Edison

Embarking on the next leg of our entrepreneurial odyssey with "Unicorn Manifesto," we dive into the crucible where all ventures begin: the genesis of an idea. In this chapter, "Igniting the Flame: Ideation and Validation," we are not merely discussing concepts in the abstract; we are setting the stage for the birthing of enterprises that alter the contours of markets and societies alike.

Ideation, the art of birthing ideas, serves as the bedrock upon which empires are built. Yet, an idea, no matter how brilliant, demands rigorous validation to ensure its viability in the tumultuous waters of the market. It's here, at this confluence of creativity and scrutiny, that the future unicorns begin to gallop.

We embark on a journey through the landscape of ideation, traversing the realms of imagination, innovation, and insight.

Every entrepreneur stands as a beacon of potential, their mind a crucible for ideas that can reshape our world. Yet, it is the act of validation—of testing, refining, and affirming these ideas—that transforms the ephemeral into the tangible, the dream into reality.

In this chapter, we illuminate the pathways through which ideas are nurtured and validated. From the spark of inspiration in Julia Silva's EcoBrush awakening to the revolutionary educational paradigms of Anika Patel's Virtual Reality Language School, we explore the narratives of those who have walked the path before us. These tales are not just stories; they are blueprints, laden with wisdom, caution, and the exhilaration of breakthroughs.

Ideation without validation is like a ship without a rudder; it might float but lacks direction. Validation acts as the compass that guides the entrepreneur through the fog of uncertainty, ensuring that their vision is not just a mirage but a beacon of innovation and utility.

As we delve into the dynamics of ideation and validation, we invite you to engage with these concepts not as mere observers but as active participants. The journey from ideation to validation is both a science and an art, requiring a blend of creativity, critical thinking, and courage.

So, dear reader, as you stand at the precipice of creation, ready to ignite the flame of your own entrepreneurial venture, remember: every great journey begins with a single step—a step of ideation, followed by the steadfast stride of validation. Are you prepared to embark on this voyage of discovery and determination? Let us ignite the flame together, illuminating the path from the spark of an idea to the beacon of success.

Opening Anecdote: EcoBrush Awakening: Julia Silva's Sustainable Revolution

Julia Silva's 'EcoBrush' Revolution In a world overwhelmed by plastic waste, Julia Silva's sustainable brainchild emerged. Her idea wasn't just another eco-friendly product; it became a movement, demonstrating the significance of marrying passion with market need, and the power of diligent validation.

Ideation: The Seed of All Startups

Before any company hits the stock market, before any product reaches the shelves, there's an idea. But how does one differentiate between a fleeting thought and a potentially groundbreaking concept? Here we delve into the anatomy of ideation.

The Birth of an Idea: Ideation Unleashed

Ideas don't pop out of thin air; they're often born from a mix of personal experiences, identified needs, and, occasionally, frustration. It's essential to feed your brain with diverse stimuli—books, conversations, travel, and more. Cultivating a mindset of curiosity and remaining observant can birth countless innovative concepts.

> **Quick Thought:**
> *Ideas are like flames; they require oxygen to grow. The oxygen here is your continuous effort in nurturing, refining, and challenging them.*

Entrepreneurship in Action: Key Ingredients

- **Expertise and Passion Intersection:** Recognize the sweet spot where your skills and passions overlap with market demands. This is your goldmine.
- **Creative Thinking Techniques:** Break the mold. Techniques like mind mapping, brainstorming sessions, or even casual discussions can lead to groundbreaking ideas.
- **Incremental Innovation:** It's not always about reinventing the wheel. A simple twist, a slight enhancement, can revolutionize industries.

Case Study Highlight: Julia Silva's 'EcoBrush' Revolution

The Birth of EcoBrush: Julia Silva, while vacationing on a Brazilian beach, noticed a recurring pattern of washed-up plastic toothbrushes among the myriad of ocean debris. An environmentalist at heart, the sight was more than just disturbing to Julia; it was a call to action. She realized that while many had begun the switch to sustainable options in various areas, daily essentials like toothbrushes were largely ignored.

Fusion of Tradition and Innovation: Instead of merely replicating the few existing eco-friendly brushes, Julia took a unique approach. She collaborated with local artisans in Brazil to incorporate traditional craftsmanship techniques. By utilizing locally sourced bamboo, a renewable resource, and natural plant-based bristles, EcoBrush became a harmonious blend of tradition and modern sustainable design.

Engaging the Audience: Julia believed that feedback-driven evolution was paramount. Launching a pilot program, she distributed the first batch of EcoBrushes to a varied demographic, from college students to elderly individuals. This not only helped her understand the product's reception but also gather insights into potential improvements.

From Idea to Revolution: The EcoBrush wasn't just another product in the market; it was a statement. Julia's dedication to environmental consciousness, combined with her relentless pursuit of perfection based on real-world feedback, led to a product that was both efficient and sustainable. Today, the EcoBrush has not just reduced plastic waste but has also raised awareness about the importance of sustainable living.

Case Study Highlight: Anika Patel's Virtual Reality Language School

The Visionary Concept: Anika Patel, having grown up in a multicultural British-Indian household, was always fascinated by languages. With advancements in Virtual Reality (VR), she envisioned a groundbreaking method of teaching languages. Anika dreamt of a VR classroom, where learners would immerse themselves in a foreign land, learning not just the language but also the culture.

Initial Stumbles: The early model of LinguaVR was purely tech-driven, focusing solely on the immersive experience. Users would virtually stroll through the streets of Paris or Tokyo, interacting with AI-driven characters in scripted scenarios. However, during beta testing, Anika discovered a significant flaw. Users missed the human touch. They wanted to converse, ask questions, and engage with real individuals, not just programmed characters.

Pivoting with Purpose: Based on the overwhelming feedback, Anika took a bold step. Instead of relying solely on AI, she integrated a feature where learners could have real-time VR chats with native language mentors from around the world. This not only made the learning experience more interactive but also bridged cultural gaps, fostering global connections.

LinguaVR Today: Anika's ability to adapt and evolve her model based on genuine user needs transformed LinguaVR from just another tech startup to a global language-learning sensation. With users spanning continents, the platform stands as a testament to how technology, when combined with human interaction, can reshape traditional learning landscapes.

Validation: Ensuring Your Flame Has Fuel

It's not enough to have a brilliant idea. Validation ensures there's a market, a genuine need. This phase saves entrepreneurs from costly mistakes and wasted effort, guiding the ideation towards a sustainable and profitable path.

```
Pro Tip: Remember, the market is vast. Your product
or service might cater to a niche, but within that
niche, it should be indispensable.
```

Dance of Creation and Confirmation

The dynamic interplay between ideation and validation isn't linear. Ideas evolve, sometimes even pivot, based on the insights from validation. Entrepreneurs must be ready to adapt, refine, and, if necessary, reinvent.

Exercise: Ideation to Validation Workshop

Ideation Exercise: Unleash Your Creative Spark

1. **Idea Generation Marathon**: Set aside 30 minutes of uninterrupted time. Using a timer, challenge yourself to write down as many business ideas as possible, no matter how outlandish they may seem. Aim for quantity over quality; this exercise is designed to unlock your creative potential and push beyond conventional boundaries.

2. **The Intersection Analysis**: Reflect on your list of ideas and identify any that sit at the intersection of your personal passions, skills, and market needs. Select the top three ideas that resonate most strongly with you and have the potential to address a genuine problem or gap in the market.

3. **Mind Map Your Ideas**: For each of the three ideas, create a mind map that explores potential applications, target audiences, and unique selling propositions. This visual representation can help you see connections and opportunities you might have missed.

Validation Exercise: Testing the Waters

1. **Hypothesis Development**: For each idea, develop a clear hypothesis that you can test. This might be about the problem your idea solves, the market demand, or the feasibility of your solution. Write your hypotheses in a testable format: "If [action], then [outcome]."

2. **Minimum Viable Research**: Conduct basic research to validate your hypotheses. This could involve:

- **Surveys**: Create a short survey to gauge interest or pain points related to your idea. Tools like Google Forms or SurveyMonkey can be helpful.
- **Interviews**: Reach out to potential customers for informal interviews to gather insights about their needs and reactions to your idea.
- **Secondary Research**: Utilize online resources, industry reports, and existing data to support or refute your hypotheses.

1. **Prototype Feedback Loop**: For the idea that passes the Minimum Viable Research phase, sketch a simple prototype or outline of the solution. Share this with a small group of potential users or peers for feedback. Focus on understanding whether your solution addresses the problem effectively and how it could be improved.

Reflection and Iteration:

- **Insight Journaling**: After completing the exercises, take some time to journal your reflections. What did you learn about your ideas through this process? Were there any surprises or new insights that emerged?
- **Next Steps Plan**: Based on the feedback and your reflections, outline the next steps for your most viable idea. Consider what you would need to move forward with a more detailed prototype, a business plan, or further market research.

Challenge For You:
Are you ready to light the entrepreneurial torch? Ideate a

product or service. Next, step into your potential customer's shoes. Would you buy it? Why or why not? Use this introspection as the initial step in your validation process.

Coming Up Next:

A solid idea is your foundation, but the building process is just beginning. Chapter 3 will architect the next layer – framing your business blueprint, understanding your audience's core, and crafting a value proposition that stands out.

3

Constructing Your Blueprint: Building a Foundational Framework

"Success always comes when preparation meets opportunity."
— Henry Hartman

With the flames of ideation and validation now burning brightly, it's time to architect the structure upon which your entrepreneurial vision will rise. "Constructing Your Blueprint: Building a Foundational Framework" marks a pivotal juncture in your journey, transitioning from the ethereal realm of ideas to the tangible process of creation. In this chapter, we delve into the essence of building a business blueprint, a compass in the ever-evolving landscape of entrepreneurship.

The business blueprint serves not merely as a plan but as a living document, a testament to the adaptability and resilience required in the fast-paced world of startups. Like the master builders of yore, today's entrepreneurs must draft their visions with both precision and flexibility, anticipating the shifts and swells of the market seas.

Through the lens of visionary ventures like Dropbox and

Slack, we explore the nuanced art of constructing a blueprint that withstands the tests of time and turbulence. These stories are not just narratives of success but are imbued with strategic insights, serving as a guide for navigating the complexities of the entrepreneurial ecosystem.

The creation of a business blueprint is akin to charting a map for an expedition; it requires an understanding of the terrain, the foresight to identify pitfalls, and the wisdom to leverage opportunities. As we journey through this chapter, we will dissect the components of a successful blueprint, from the Lean Canvas Approach to the articulation of a Unique Value Proposition (UVP) that distinguishes your venture in a crowded marketplace.

But remember, the true essence of a blueprint lies in its capacity for evolution. It's a dynamic framework, one that embraces change and adapts with agility. This chapter encourages you to think of your blueprint not as a rigid set of plans but as a flexible strategy, ready to pivot in response to new insights and opportunities.

Opening Anecdote: Dropbox's Visionary Insight

Before cloud storage transformed our digital lifestyles, there was a challenge of file synchronization. Dropbox, under the leadership of Drew Houston, envisioned a solution. But rather than diving in with an exhaustive product, they started with a concise, clear vision: a video MVP. This video wasn't just promotional; it emphasized the core problem and elegantly proposed the solution. The result? An explosive overnight interest.

15

Understanding the Business Blueprint in a Rapid-Changing World

Entrepreneurship is a dynamic journey. As startups navigate through this vibrant ecosystem, having a foundational blueprint becomes imperative. And in today's agile landscape, this blueprint is more about adaptability than rigidity.

> **Quick Thought:**
> *A business blueprint is not a fixed roadmap but a flexible guide, adapting to feedback, market shifts, and evolving visions.*

Entrepreneurship in Action: Key Ingredients

- **The Lean Canvas Approach:** Transcending traditional, exhaustive business plans, the Lean Canvas offers a concise snapshot, ensuring that startups remain nimble and focused.
- **Audience Insights:** Beyond demographics lies the treasure trove of motivations, challenges, and aspirations. Deep diving into these insights ensures that your solution resonates profoundly.
- **Unique Value Proposition (UVP):** In a sea of solutions, your UVP is the lighthouse. It needs to be clear, compelling, and resonate with the problem you're addressing.

Case Study Highlight: Slack - The Unexpected MVP Evolution

Genesis of an Idea: Stewart Butterfield's initial venture was a multiplayer online game named "Glitch." For effective team communication during its development, they created a chat tool. Little did they know that this mere internal tool would overshadow the game itself.

The Pivot: As "Glitch" faced challenges and was eventually shuttered, the team took time to introspect. Among the ashes of their failed game, the glimmer of their chat tool remained undeniable. They recognized its broader application - a platform that could revolutionize workplace communication beyond just game development.

Refining for the Market: Stewart and his team didn't just release their internal tool as-is. They enhanced and refined it, introducing features tailored to businesses of all sizes. Slack became more than just a messaging app; it provided channels, integrations, and features that addressed pain points in contemporary office communication.

Slack's Dominance: The pivot from "Glitch" to Slack is an iconic tale of entrepreneurial adaptability. Today, Slack isn't just another tool but a staple in businesses worldwide. Its journey exemplifies that sometimes, success lies not in your primary vision but in the peripheral solutions you create along the way.

Case Study: Dropbox - Simple Yet Profound

A Universal Dilemma: Drew Houston found himself in a familiar predicament many faced – forgetting his USB flash drive. This moment of frustration led to a eureka realization: the need for seamless, cloud-based file synchronization.

The Power of Demonstration: Instead of diving straight into a fully-fledged product, Drew took an unconventional approach. He created a straightforward video MVP that depicted the simplicity and utility of Dropbox. By focusing on common pain points, he didn't just showcase software but a solution to a universal problem.

Overwhelming Response: The video MVP did wonders. Without a tangible product, Dropbox's waitlist skyrocketed from a mere 5,000 to a staggering 75,000 sign-ups overnight. The clarity and relatability of the video resonated with a broad audience, validating Houston's idea on an unimaginable scale.

Dropbox's Evolution: Drew's vision, coupled with the astounding market response, led to Dropbox's rapid development. Today, it stands as one of the most used cloud storage solutions globally. Drew's journey underscores that sometimes, the most profound impacts come from addressing basic needs with elegance and simplicity.

```
Pro Tip: Embrace agility. A business blueprint is not
set in stone. As market feedback and insights roll
in, be ready to iterate and refine.
```

The Art of Constructive Blueprinting

Constructing a business blueprint is both an art and science. While it provides structure and clarity, it also demands flexibility. The essence? Stay adaptive, focused, and always be in tune with your market.

Exercise: Blueprint Building Workshop

Developing Your Business Blueprint:

1. **Lean Canvas Deep Dive**: Using the Lean Canvas tool as your guide, dedicate a session to thoroughly complete each segment of the canvas for your startup idea. This exercise is not just about filling in boxes but understanding the underlying strategy and assumptions of your business model. Focus on areas like your unique value proposition, customer segments, channels, and revenue streams. Aim for specificity and clarity.

2. **Audience Mapping**: Create detailed profiles for three distinct segments of your target market. Go beyond demographics to explore psychographics—what motivates them, their fears, needs, and how your product or service fits into their lives. Use tools like the Persona Generator for a more nuanced understanding.

3. **UVP Refinement Workshop**: Craft a clear and compelling unique value proposition for your startup. This should succinctly communicate the unique benefit your product or service offers to your target market. Then, challenge yourself further by distilling this UVP into a single, impactful sentence. Share this with at least three people unfamiliar with your project and gauge their

reaction—does it resonate and spark interest?

Validation through Engagement:

1. **Feedback Collection Strategy**: Design a structured plan to collect feedback on your business blueprint. This could involve surveys, interviews, or focus groups with potential customers. Identify key questions you need answers to, focusing on validating the assumptions in your Lean Canvas.
2. **Competitive Analysis Table**: Create a table comparing your startup with three direct competitors. Include factors such as UVP, customer segments, pricing, and distribution channels. Analyze where your offering stands out and where you face the most significant challenges.
3. **Scenario Planning Session**: Conduct a scenario planning exercise to anticipate potential shifts in your business landscape. Identify at least three "what if" scenarios (e.g., a new competitor enters the market, a change in customer behavior, a technological breakthrough) and outline how your business blueprint would adapt to each.

Reflection and Next Steps:

- **Insight Journaling**: After completing the exercises, spend some time reflecting on what you have learned. How has your understanding of your business blueprint evolved? Are there areas that require further research or adjustment?
- **Action Plan for Refinement**: Based on the feedback and insights gathered, outline a set of actionable steps you can take to refine your business blueprint. This might

include further market research, prototype development, or revising your business model.

Challenge For You:

In the coming week, refine your startup's UVP. Seek feedback from potential users. Does it resonate? Does it stand out? Fine-tune based on the feedback.

Coming Up Next:

We dive into the transformation from blueprint to tangible product, unraveling the intricacies of bringing an MVP to life.

4

Constructing Your MVP: From Blueprint to Reality

"The key is not to prioritize what's on your schedule,
but to schedule your priorities."
— Stephen R. Covey

With the architectural blueprint of your venture in hand, we now pivot towards one of the most exhilarating phases of the entrepreneurial journey—bringing your Minimum Viable Product (MVP) from concept to reality. In "Constructing Your MVP: From Blueprint to Reality," we bridge the gap between the strategic framework you've meticulously crafted and the tangible expression of your vision.

The creation of an MVP is a pivotal moment that encapsulates the essence of entrepreneurship: the transformation of ideas into tangible solutions that address real-world needs. Here, we distill the core functionality of your product or service, ensuring that it not only exists but thrives in the marketplace.

Through the lens of transformative stories like Airbnb's strategic pivot and Slack's unexpected evolution, we unravel the mystique of the MVP. These narratives are not mere success stories; they are proof of the MVP's power to validate, adapt, and catalyze growth through focused iteration and user feedback.

Demystifying the MVP goes beyond recognizing it as a buzzword. It's an approach that champions pragmatism, allowing you to test hypotheses, minimize risks, and engage directly with your audience. By prioritizing your product's core value, you create a foundation for meaningful interaction and continuous refinement.

As we navigate the construction of your MVP, we emphasize the critical ingredients for success: a crystal-clear objective, identification of essential features, and the establishment of a feedback loop. These components are not just steps but principles, guiding you towards an MVP that resonates deeply with your target users.

Opening Anecdote: The Airbnb Revelation

In the early days of Airbnb, the founders were grappling with a stagnant growth rate. As we'll explore later in our case study, a pivotal decision to enhance the quality of property photos made a monumental difference. This wasn't about changing the platform's core; it was about enhancing the user experience. The result was a transformative boost to their user base. The Airbnb story underlines the might of MVP — pinpointing and optimizing key elements that can redefine business trajectories.

Demystifying the MVP: More than Just a Buzzword

The Real MVP

An MVP, or Minimum Viable Product, is your product's essence, stripped of any frills, yet entirely functional and value-adding. While some mistakenly consider it an unfinished version of the product, it's truly about launching with the vital core, grasping real-world feedback, and refining.

Why MVP?

• **Risk Reduction**: A well-defined MVP lets you test waters without diving deep. If changes are required, they can be done without colossal shifts.

• **Cost Efficiency**: MVPs steer focus to what's crucial, enabling optimal resource allocation.

• **User-Centric**: By centering around the main value proposition, MVPs ensure that the product genuinely addresses user needs.

> ### *Quick Thought:*
> *The MVP philosophy stands as a beacon amidst the stormy seas of entrepreneurship, guiding the way with clarity and purpose.*

Entrepreneurship in Action: Key Ingredients

• **Crystal Clear Objective**: It's paramount to comprehend the pain point or need you're addressing. Can you articulate it in a sentence?

• **Essential Features**: MVP isn't about trimming down

to mediocrity but distilling to excellence. Identify core functionalities that best address the objective.
- **Feedback Loop**: Your MVP is a living entity. As it interfaces with real users, gather insights, understand pain points, and be ready to adapt.

Scaling Your MVP: Growth Through Iteration

Once your MVP takes flight, remember that this is the beginning of a dynamic journey. Feedback isn't just information; it's the lifeblood that will nourish your MVP's evolution.

Case Study Highlight: Slack (yes, again!)- Pivoting Towards Success through MVP

The Genesis of Glitch: Stewart Butterfield's primary intention was not to revolutionize workplace communication but to entertain with a unique multiplayer online game named "Glitch." This ambitious project, however, faced unexpected roadblocks and challenges.

The Accidental Discovery: Amidst the development of "Glitch," the team required a robust and efficient communication tool. This internal tool's efficacy didn't escape Butterfield's observation, and the potential for a broader market began to crystallize in his mind.

The MVP and Evolution of Slack: With "Glitch" fading into the background, the focus shifted to this internal tool. The MVP for Slack was simple – streamline and optimize team communication. As early adopters began to use Slack, feedback was religiously collected. It wasn't long before integrations with third-party tools were introduced, adding layers of functionality but retaining its core promise: seamless communication.

The Impact of Slack: From its inadvertent origins to setting the gold standard for workplace communication tools, Slack is a testament to the power of recognizing potential and the value of the MVP approach. In a landscape dotted with communication tools, Slack carved its niche, reshaping how teams collaborate and converse.

Case Study: Airbnb - From Humble Beginnings to Global Disruption via MVP

A Crisis and A Conference: In the backdrop of a popular design conference in San Francisco, Brian Chesky and Joe Gebbia faced a personal financial challenge – making rent. Merging their imminent need with the city's lack of accommodation due to the conference, they decided to rent out their living space, laying the foundation stone for Airbnb.

The First Iteration: The concept was simple. Offer attendees an authentic local experience in their living room, complete with breakfast. The response was surprisingly positive, signaling that they might be onto something bigger than just a temporary rent solution.

Evolving with Feedback: As Airbnb started gaining traction, the importance of user feedback became abundantly clear. One significant insight was the influence of property photos on booking rates. This led to Airbnb offering professional photography services to hosts, significantly boosting trust and consequently, reservations.

The Global Phenomenon: Today, Airbnb isn't just another accommodation platform; it's a cultural and economic disruptor. Its growth story epitomizes the MVP principle: start with a basic, genuine solution and evolve relentlessly based on user feedback. With millions of listings worldwide, Airbnb's journey from a San Francisco apartment to global dominance demonstrates the magic of aligning user needs with business evolution.

```
Pro Tip: Your MVP is like clay. Start with a basic
shape (idea) and then mold, refine, and enhance as
you gather insights from your audience.
```

Are You Ready to MVP?

Embracing the MVP mindset means understanding the elegance of simplicity. It's not about offering less, but offering what matters most. Remember Airbnb's photo tweak or Slack's unexpected pivot? Small insights can lead to seismic shifts.

Exercise: MVP Creation Workshop

Conceptualizing and Refining Your MVP:

1. **MVP Blueprint**: Drawing from your business blueprint, isolate the core value your product or service offers. Sketch a basic prototype or service outline that embodies this value. Focus on simplicity—what is the minimum you need to test your key hypotheses about customer needs and product-market fit?

2. **Feature Prioritization Matrix**: Create a matrix to

prioritize features based on their importance to your customers and their feasibility for your team. This will help you identify the "must-have" features for your MVP. Use criteria such as customer value, differentiation from competitors, and implementation complexity.

3. **Iterative Feedback Loop Setup**: Design a plan for collecting and integrating feedback. This should include defining your feedback channels (e.g., user interviews, surveys, digital analytics), setting a schedule for review sessions, and establishing metrics for success. Remember, the goal of your MVP is learning as much as possible, as quickly as possible.

Validation Through Engagement:

1. **Hypothesis Testing Plan**: For each core feature or aspect of your MVP, develop a clear, testable hypothesis. For example, "If we include feature X, then user engagement will increase by Y%." Outline how you will test these hypotheses through user interactions with your MVP.

2. **Mockup and User Story Creation**: Utilize tools like Balsamiq or Sketch to create mockups of your MVP. Then, craft user stories that describe how your target customer will interact with your MVP. This exercise helps visualize the user journey and identify any potential friction points.

3. **Early Adopter Recruitment**: Identify channels through which you can recruit early adopters for your MVP testing. Consider leveraging social media, industry forums, or personal networks. Develop a pitch that communicates the value of participating in your MVP testing, focusing on the exclusive opportunity to shape the product.

Reflection and Adaptation:

- **Insight Diary**: After conducting the exercises, maintain an "Insight Diary" for at least two weeks during the MVP testing phase. Note observations, user feedback, and any unexpected outcomes. Use this diary to track how your understanding of the customer and product evolves.
- **Adaptation Plan**: Based on the feedback and insights collected, draft an adaptation plan for your MVP. This should outline potential pivots, feature revisions, or additional hypotheses to test. The plan should be flexible, allowing for quick iteration based on ongoing user feedback.

Challenge For You:

In the coming week, identify a singular enhancement in your product (or idea) that could potentially be your game-changer.

Coming Up Next:

The next chapter beckons with a deep dive into the art and science of feedback interpretation, an essential compass for your MVP journey.

5

Set Sail: Launch and Early Growth

"Success usually comes to those who are too busy to be looking for it."
— Henry David Thoreau

Embarking upon the voyage from conceptualization to market presence, "Set Sail: Launch and Early Growth" is the beacon that guides your startup out of the harbor and into the open sea of entrepreneurial endeavor. This chapter is the culmination of your preparation, a testament to your readiness to introduce your vision to the world and chart a course through the uncharted waters of market acceptance and growth.

As we delve into the essence of a successful launch, we recognize it as more than a mere debut; it's a crucial opportunity to make an indelible mark on your intended audience, setting the tone for everything that follows. The stories of Spotify's strategic ingenuity and Uber's market adaptation serve not just as inspiration but as a blueprint for navigating the early stages of growth with agility and foresight.

The launch phase is a multifaceted endeavor, encompassing strategic positioning, effective communication, and the establishment of robust feedback mechanisms. It's a period characterized by learning, adapting, and iterating, where the feedback from your first users becomes the cornerstone of continuous improvement and expansion.

Through a mix of strategic insights and actionable exercises, this chapter equips you with the tools to craft a compelling launch message, identify and understand your audience, and establish pathways for collecting and integrating user feedback. As you set sail with your MVP, remember that the journey ahead is both exhilarating and demanding, requiring a captain's resolve and a navigator's precision.

Opening Anecdote: Spotify's Swift Surge

When Spotify first launched in 2008, they had a simple goal: combat piracy by offering a better experience. They entered a market dominated by giants like iTunes and pirate platforms. Instead of creating just another music purchase platform, Spotify turned to streaming, creating a unique, user-friendly experience that emphasized discovery and access. This shift in approach saw them grow swiftly and dominate the music streaming industry, underlining the importance of a well-prepared launch and the magic of adaptability.

The Power of the First Impression: The Launch Essence

A product's launch isn't just an announcement; it's a statement of intent. It's about capturing attention, carving out a niche, and most importantly, setting the stage for subsequent interactions with your audience.

Why a Strong Launch?

- **Momentum Builder:** A good launch gives you an initial thrust, propelling you forward.
- **Brand Positioning:** First impressions shape perceptions. A solid launch can set the tone for your brand's identity.
- **Validation and Feedback:** Early adopters can provide invaluable insights and validate your core assumptions.

> *Quick Thought:*
> *While launching feels like a singular event, its ripples can have lasting effects on a startup's trajectory.*

Entrepreneurship in Action: Key Ingredients

- **Strategic Positioning:** Identify where you want to be in the minds of your consumers.
- **Effective Communication:** Craft a message that resonates, informs, and compels.
- **Feedback Mechanisms:** Have tools in place to capture initial reactions, feedback, and areas of improvement.

Riding the Growth Wave: From Launch to Expansion

A product's journey is much like sailing. The launch sets the direction, but it's the constant adjustment to the winds (market dynamics) that ensures you reach your destination.

Case Study: Uber - Navigating Growth's Twists and Turns

Starting with a Premium Promise: Uber's inception wasn't as a solution to everyday commuting but as a luxury car service for the elite of San Francisco. The initial model focused on exclusivity, providing a premium experience that was miles apart from traditional taxi services.

Recognizing the Broader Appeal: As Uber's user base started to swell, data and feedback revealed a consistent desire for a more approachable, affordable version of their service. This meant transcending their original brand proposition and venturing into more democratic urban transport solutions.

The Introduction of UberX: Responding to the demand, Uber launched UberX, which allowed non-professional drivers to offer rides in their private vehicles at significantly lower rates. This shift wasn't just an addition to their services; it signaled a paradigm change, democratizing ride-hailing for everyone.

The Global Urban Mobility Revolution: Uber's relentless pursuit of innovation, backed by data and user feedback, has continually disrupted the transportation sector. From integrating food delivery with UberEats to exploring aerial transport with Uber Elevate, Uber's story is a testament to the power of adaptive evolution based on customer feedback.

Case Study: Canva - Melanie Perkins' Visionary Canvas

The Seeds of an Idea: Melanie Perkins, an entrepreneur of Asian descent, initiated her journey with "Fusion Books" during her college days. This platform allowed students to design and print custom yearbooks. The success of "Fusion Books" sowed the seeds for a more expansive vision: democratizing design.

The Birth of Canva: Recognizing the broader need for an easy-to-use design platform, Perkins co-founded Canva. The MVP was clear: A drag-and-drop design tool that could empower anyone, regardless of their design proficiency, to create professional-quality graphics.

Iterative Growth and Expansion: As users flocked to Canva, Perkins and her team listened. They expanded beyond the initial offering to introduce features like Canva Print, Canva for Education, and even an enterprise version. Each step was a response to real user needs, ensuring Canva remained relevant and invaluable.

The Billion-Dollar Design Platform: Today, Canva stands as a unicorn startup, with a valuation exceeding billions. Its expansive template library, coupled with intuitive tools, has made it the go-to platform for design needs globally. Perkins' story is an inspiring narrative of spotting a genuine need, starting small, and scaling with intent.

```
Pro Tip: Growth is multidimensional. Sometimes, it's
not just about more users, but deeper engagement,
expanded services, or entering new markets.
```

Setting Sail with Confidence

Launching is both an end and a beginning. It's the culmination of pre-launch efforts and the start of a new journey. By positioning well, engaging users, and iterating based on feedback, you're not just setting sail; you're navigating towards success.

Exercise: Launch Preparation and Early Growth Strategy

Preparing for Launch:

1. **Launch Message Workshop**: Craft the core message of your launch, encapsulating the essence of your startup and its value proposition in a single, compelling sentence. This message should be memorable, succinct, and convey the unique benefit your product or service offers.

2. **Target Audience Analysis**: Identify and document detailed profiles for at least three key segments of your target audience. For each segment, delve into their motivations, challenges, and how your offering provides a solution. Utilize tools like the Persona Generator to add depth and realism to these profiles.

3. **Feedback Collection System Design**: Develop a systematic approach for collecting, analyzing, and acting on user feedback post-launch. This might include setting up digital feedback forms, social media listening tools, and regular review meetings with your team to evaluate feedback trends and identify actionable insights.

Navigating Early Growth:

1. **Market Adaptation Plan**: Given the dynamic nature of the startup ecosystem, outline a strategy for how your venture will adapt to market feedback and emerging trends. Include mechanisms for staying informed about industry developments and competitor moves, as well as a process for regularly revisiting and revising your business model based on this intelligence.

2. **Growth Metrics Dashboard Setup**: Identify key metrics that will indicate success in your early growth phase. These could include user acquisition rates, engagement metrics, customer lifetime value, and churn rate, among others. Use tools like Google Analytics, Mixpanel, or a custom dashboard to monitor these metrics closely.

3. **Early Adopter Engagement Plan**: Design a program to identify, engage, and leverage early adopters of your product or service. This could involve creating an exclusive community for early users, offering special incentives for feedback, and using their stories and testimonials to attract broader audiences.

Reflection and Iteration:

- **Launch Diary**: Maintain a "Launch Diary" for the first month post-launch, recording observations, successes, challenges, and unexpected outcomes. Use this diary to capture the lessons learned and emotions experienced during this critical phase.

- **Growth Strategy Review Session**: Schedule a strategy review session with your team one month post-launch. Use the insights gathered from your Launch Diary and Growth Metrics Dashboard to evaluate the effectiveness of your launch and early growth strategies. Identify what worked, what didn't, and what adjustments are needed to continue on a trajectory of sustainable growth.

Challenge For You:

Post-launch, identify one key insight or piece of feedback every day for a week. At week's end, analyze the trends and devise an action plan.

Coming Up Next:

Let's unpack the complexities of scaling. As growth accelerates, how do you manage challenges and seize opportunities? Dive in and discover.

6

Scaling to New Heights: Operational Growth and Expansion

"Growth is never by mere chance; it is the result of forces working together."
— James Cash Penney

As we pivot from the initial surge of launch and early growth to the ambitious realms of scaling, "Scaling to New Heights: Operational Growth and Expansion" serves as your guide through the multifaceted landscape of elevating your startup to new echelons. Scaling is not merely an increase in numbers but a harmonious expansion of your venture's core elements—its culture, operations, and market presence—ensuring sustainable growth and resilience in the face of evolving market demands.

Netflix's transformative journey from a DVD rental service to a streaming behemoth epitomizes the essence of visionary scaling. It illustrates that true scaling often requires reimagining your business model in anticipation of future trends and consumer behaviors, thereby securing a competitive edge in a rapidly changing digital landscape.

This chapter delves into the intricacies of scaling beyond mere numerical growth, focusing on the qualitative aspects that ensure sustained success and stability. It's about building a robust infrastructure that supports expansion, cultivating leadership that inspires and adapts, and fostering a culture that thrives on innovation and feedback.

Through strategic insights, practical exercises, and illuminating case studies of Shopify's ecosystem-driven growth and Zappos's culture-centric expansion, we explore how to scale your operations while maintaining the quality, ethos, and agility that marked your early days.

Opening Anecdote: Netflix's Visionary Voyage

At its inception, Netflix was a DVD-by-mail service, a seemingly simple operation. However, recognizing the potential of online streaming ahead of many competitors, Netflix made a paradigm shift. Scaling wasn't just about reaching more mailboxes, but revolutionizing how we consume entertainment. Their story underlines the importance of visionary scaling: adapting to technological possibilities and audience behavior, even when it means reimagining your business model.

Understanding the Scale-Up: Growth Beyond Numbers

Scaling, while often equated to numerical growth, is an intricate dance of maintaining quality, culture, and efficiency, even as you expand boundaries. It's about anticipating challenges before they loom large and preparing your venture to glide over potential pitfalls.

Why Scale-Up Matters?

- **Market Penetration:** It enables your startup to reach a broader audience.
- **Resource Allocation:** As the team and tasks grow, effective resource management becomes crucial.
- **Innovation:** Larger operations often have more means to invest in R&D and innovation.

> ### Quick Thought:
> *Scaling is like climbing a mountain. It's not just about reaching the peak but ensuring the journey upwards strengthens and doesn't deplete.*

Entrepreneurship in Action: Key Ingredients

- **Adaptive Infrastructure:** Anticipate growth and ensure that your infrastructure can adapt without massive overhauls.
- **Engaged Leadership:** A team looking to grow needs leaders who are deeply engaged, not just at the strategic level but in the trenches, understanding daily operations.
- **Feedback Loops:** As operations expand, maintain mechanisms to capture feedback both internally (from employees) and externally (customers).

The Human Factor: Teams and Culture in Scale-Ups

The exponential growth of startups often means teams multiply. Maintaining a cohesive, motivated, and efficient team as numbers swell is a testament to effective leadership and robust company culture.

Case Study: Shopify - Ecosystem as a Catalyst for Growth

From Specific Solution to Broad Platform: Shopify's inception was grounded in a simple pain point: the complexities of setting up an online store. It started as a streamlined solution for entrepreneurs wanting to sell online without the technical hassles.

Embracing Integration: As Shopify's user base grew, the team recognized that each business had unique needs that couldn't be addressed by a one-size-fits-all platform. Thus, they allowed third-party developers to create apps that merchants could integrate into their stores. This approach not only enriched the platform but also created new revenue streams and solutions for niche problems.

Building a Community: Beyond software, Shopify nurtured a community of store owners, developers, and partners. By hosting events, providing educational content, and even launching a fund for app developers, they ensured that their growth was intertwined with the success of their community.

A Global E-commerce Powerhouse: Today, Shopify isn't just an e-commerce platform; it's an ecosystem where businesses of all sizes can thrive. Their growth isn't just reflected in numbers but in the myriad of entrepreneurs they empower daily.

Case Study: Zappos - Defining Growth Beyond Revenue

A Commitment to Culture: At the heart of Zappos's success wasn't just selling shoes online, but a profound commitment to creating a remarkable company culture. Tony Hsieh, their CEO, was convinced that while products could be replicated, a strong, unique culture couldn't.

Customer Service as the North Star: Zappos set the bar high in online retail, offering perks like free shipping and 365-day returns. But beyond policies, they empowered their customer service reps to genuinely engage with and delight customers, creating memorable shopping experiences.

The "Pay to Quit" Philosophy: As Zappos expanded, maintaining their culture became a challenge. To address this, they introduced a "pay to quit" policy, offering new hires a monetary incentive to leave if they felt misaligned with the company's culture. It was a bold move, ensuring only those genuinely aligned with Zappos's ethos stayed.

Scaling with Heart: Zappos's journey stands as a lesson in values-driven growth. Their consistent focus on culture and customer service ensured that even as they scaled to become a billion-dollar company, they remained as customer-centric and employee-friendly as a small startup.

```
Pro Tip: Scaling introduces complexity, but the
essence remains the same. As you grow, revisit your
startup's core values and ensure they are reflected
in every new dimension you add.
```

The Zenith Awaits, But Relish the Ascent

Scaling is as much about the journey as the destination. While the allure of rapid growth is intoxicating, true success lies in growing sustainably, ensuring every new height achieved is on a solid foundation.

Exercise: Strategic Scaling Workshop

Planning for Scalable Growth:

1. **Scalability Audit**: Conduct an audit of your startup's current operations, focusing on three key areas: technology/platform, team structure, and customer support processes. For each area, evaluate scalability by asking, "Can this aspect of our business handle a tenfold increase in customers without a proportional increase in resources?" Document your findings and identify potential bottlenecks.

2. **Role Evolution Plan**: As your startup scales, the roles and responsibilities within your team will evolve. Map out the critical roles you anticipate needing in the next phase of growth. Consider how existing roles will evolve and what new roles may need to be created. Include skills and attributes necessary for these future roles, focusing on adaptability, leadership, and specialization.

3. **Feedback Loop Enhancement**: Design an advanced feedback collection and analysis system that can scale with your business. This might include automating customer feedback collection, setting up internal feedback channels for team members, and utilizing data analytics tools to sift through feedback efficiently. Ensure this system allows

for quick adaptation based on actionable insights.

Fostering a Scalable Culture:

1. **Cultural Values Charter**: Create a charter of your startup's core cultural values, designed to remain steadfast amid growth. This exercise involves defining the principles that underpin your company culture, ways to embed these values in your operations, and strategies for maintaining this culture as your team expands.

2. **Innovation Incubation Program**: Outline a program within your company dedicated to fostering innovation as you scale. This could involve regular hackathons, a set budget for experimental projects, or a suggestion box for innovative ideas with a structured process for evaluation and implementation. The goal is to keep the entrepreneurial spirit alive, even as the organization grows.

3. **Cross-functional Team Integration Exercise**: Plan for the formation of cross-functional teams to tackle specific growth challenges or opportunities. This exercise aims to break down silos that might form as departments expand and ensure that diverse perspectives are brought to bear on strategic decisions.

Reflection and Strategic Adjustment:

- **Growth Reflection Sessions**: Schedule regular reflection sessions with your team to discuss the scaling journey. These sessions should focus on what is working, what challenges are emerging, and how the team is adapting to the demands of growth. Use these reflections to adjust your scaling strategy dynamically.

- **Scaling Playbook Creation**: Based on your experiences and the exercises above, begin drafting a "Scaling Playbook" for your startup. This document should capture best practices, lessons learned, and strategies that have worked (or not worked) as you've scaled. The playbook will be a living document, continually updated as your startup evolves.

Challenge For You:

Identify one process or aspect of your startup that's currently manual or inefficient. Brainstorm ways it could be scaled or optimized.

Coming Up Next:

We venture into the intriguing realm of startup valuations. How do you gauge your startup's worth, especially when it's not just about the numbers? Dive in to demystify the art and science of valuations.

7

Fueling the Rocket: Funding and Financing

"Opportunities don't happen. You create them."
— Chris Grosser

Embarking upon the next chapter of our entrepreneurial saga, "Fueling the Rocket: Funding and Financing" unfolds as a pivotal expedition into the financial veins that energize the heart of startup growth. With the spirit of Sara Blakely's Spanx odyssey as our muse, we traverse the multifarious avenues of acquiring capital, each path offering its own blend of challenges and triumphs. This narrative is not just about securing a financial lifeline; it's an exploration of how funding, in its many forms, can serve as a catalyst for innovation, expansion, and the realization of your entrepreneurial dreams.

As we delve into the essence of this journey, we recognize that funding is more than mere monetary gain—it's a strategic alliance, marrying your startup's vision with the resources, expertise, and networks that can propel it to uncharted territories. This chapter is a testament to the transformative power of well-orchestrated funding strategies, guiding you through the labyrinth of bootstrapping, angel investments, venture capital, and beyond.

Through a tapestry of case studies, exercises, and introspective queries, we aim to illuminate the path for navigating the complexities of funding. From the self-reliant resilience of bootstrapping to the communal embrace of crowdfunding, each funding milestone is a step towards elevating your venture to new heights. We venture together into the strategic crafting of pitches that resonate, the building of relationships that endure, and the cultivation of a funding ethos that aligns with the core of your startup's mission.

Opening Anecdote: Spanx's Self-financed Success

Sara Blakely, the founder of Spanx, started her journey with just $5,000 from her savings. Without seeking external funding, she built an empire and became the world's youngest self-made female billionaire. Her story reminds us that while external funding can accelerate growth, creativity, determination, and a strong product can also carve a path to success.

The Funding Frontier: More Than Just Money
While funding injects capital into a startup, it also brings expertise, mentorship, networks, and more. The challenge is in aligning the funding source with the startup's vision, stage, and strategic needs.

Why Does Funding Matter?
• **Acceleration:** External funding can fast-track growth and market penetration.

- **Resources:** Beyond money, investors bring knowledge, networks, and validation.
- **Risk Mitigation:** Financial stability reduces existential threats and allows focus on innovation.

> ***Quick Thought:***
> *Think of funding as the fuel for your startup's rocket. Too little and you might not reach orbit; too much, and you could burn out too quickly.*

Unpacking Funding Options:

1. **Bootstrapping:** A test of self-reliance, teaching frugality and resourcefulness.
2. **Friends and Family:** A blend of trust and professionalism is essential to maintain relationships.
3. **Angel Investors:** It's not just about money but finding mentors who resonate with your mission.
4. **Venture Capital:** High stakes, high rewards. Ensure alignment of visions and values.
5. **Crowdfunding:** A litmus test of product-market fit and an early marketing opportunity.
6. **Loans & Grants:** A classic route, requiring rigorous planning and stringent financial discipline.

Crafting Your Funding Narrative:

Investors don't invest in ideas; they invest in people and stories. Paint a vivid picture of your vision, showcasing not just the potential returns, but the journey and impact.

Case Study: Tristan Walker's 'Walker & Company' - Navigating the Funding Landscape

Starting from Scratch: Tristan Walker, much like Sara Blakely of Spanx, started with a personal problem: the absence of grooming products tailored for Black men. His solution, 'Walker & Company,' was born out of the need for a product that truly addressed the unique challenges faced by people of color.

Seed Stage: Armed with a prototype of the Bevel razor, Tristan sought initial funding. He didn't have millions at his disposal, but his passionate pitch and the obvious market gap resonated with many. His early investors weren't just check-writers; they were mentors, guiding him through the intricate world of consumer goods.

Series Funding and Growth: As 'Bevel' gained traction, Tristan realized the potential of expanding his product line. He approached venture capitalists, not just for their money but for their expertise in scaling businesses. Each round of funding was meticulously planned, ensuring that he retained control over his brand's mission and vision.

Acquisition as a Funding Strategy: The acquisition by Procter & Gamble wasn't an exit for Tristan. It was strategic. P&G provided the resources, both in terms of capital and expertise, to scale 'Walker & Company' to new heights. This acquisition underscores an essential funding lesson: always keep the long-term vision in sight.

Case Study: Arlan Hamilton's 'Backstage Capital' - Breaking Barriers in Venture Capital

Humble Beginnings: Arlan Hamilton, a gay Black woman, didn't fit the typical VC mold. Starting with no formal background in finance or connections in Silicon Valley, she had a vision: to address the glaring funding disparity faced by founders who are women, people of color, and LGBTQ.

A Vision Worth Fighting For: Arlan's journey wasn't easy. From being homeless to attending meetings at tech conferences, she persisted, driven by her conviction. She knew the statistics: a minuscule percentage of VC funding went to Black women founders. Her goal was to change this narrative, one investment at a time.

Bootstrapping to Angel Investments: In the early days, Arlan leveraged her savings, supplemented with freelance gigs, to self-fund her mission. Her passion attracted mentors and early supporters who saw potential in her vision. It wasn't just about the funds but the affirmation that her cause resonated with others.

A Unique Investment Philosophy: Backstage Capital emerged not merely as another VC firm but as a beacon of hope for minority founders. Arlan's investment thesis was simple: overlooked founders often create solutions that address unique, underserved market needs, leading to significant opportunities. And it paid off. In just a few years, Backstage Capital invested in over 100 startups, most of them led by underrepresented founders.

```
Pro Tip: When seeking funding, always emphasize the
problem you're solving, the solution's uniqueness,
and why you're the right person/team to execute the
vision.
```

The Launchpad is Just the Beginning

Securing funding is akin to preparing your startup for launch. The real journey begins post-takeoff. Fuel up wisely, understanding that the partnership with investors is a marathon, not a sprint.

Exercise: Crafting Your Funding Strategy

Evaluating Funding Avenues:

1. **Funding Landscape Analysis**: Take a deep dive into understanding the various funding options available for your startup. Create a comparative chart that evaluates bootstrapping, angel investment, venture capital, crowdfunding, and loans & grants against criteria such as speed of acquisition, level of equity relinquished, and alignment with your startup's values and goals.
2. **Readiness Checklist**: Develop a checklist to determine your startup's readiness for funding. This should include key milestones, such as a validated MVP, a clear business model, a solid pitch deck, and any initial traction or revenue. This exercise helps ensure that you approach investors or funding sources at the right time, with the right story.

3. **Investor Mapping Exercise**: Identify and research potential investors who not only align with your startup's industry but also share your vision and values. Use tools like Crunchbase to create a target list of investors, noting their past investments, focus areas, and any known investment criteria.

Preparing for Engagement:

1. **Pitch Development Workshop**: Craft your startup's pitch, focusing on storytelling that highlights the uniqueness of your idea, the problem it solves, the market potential, and why you and your team are the ones to bring this vision to life. Practice delivering this pitch in a concise one-minute version for initial encounters and a more detailed version for formal meetings.

2. **Financial Projections Model**: Build a robust financial model that projects your startup's growth over the next 3-5 years. Include revenue forecasts, expense estimates, and cash flow calculations. This model should demonstrate a clear path to profitability or significant growth, supporting your case for investment.

3. **Negotiation Role-play**: With a team member or mentor, simulate a funding negotiation to prepare for real-world discussions. Focus on aspects like valuation, equity offered, and terms of investment. This exercise aims to refine your negotiation skills, ensuring you can confidently and effectively navigate investment discussions.

Reflection and Strategy Refinement:

- **Funding Strategy Journal**: After completing the exercises, reflect on your funding strategy in a journal. Consider what you've learned about the different funding options, your startup's readiness, and the investors you aim to engage with. Use this reflection to refine your approach and identify any gaps in your preparation or areas for further research.
- **Action Plan for Funding Engagement**: Based on your analyses and preparation exercises, outline a strategic plan for engaging with potential funding sources. Set specific goals for outreach, pitch meetings, and follow-up actions. This plan should serve as a roadmap for your funding efforts, keeping you focused and proactive in your pursuit of capital.

Challenge For You:

Analyze your current financial health. If you had to pitch to investors tomorrow, what would be your three primary selling points?

Coming Up Next:

Let's dive into the realm of strategic partnerships. Beyond funding, how can collaboration unlock unprecedented growth and open doors previously unimaginable? Join us to explore this synergy.

8

Forming Alliances: Building Strategic Partnerships

"Alone we can do so little; together we can do so much."
— Helen Keller

As we journey further into the entrepreneurial cosmos, "Forming Alliances: Building Strategic Partnerships" unveils the transformative power of collaboration. Through the harmonious alliance of Starbucks and Spotify, we witness a symphony of success that transcends mere product integration to create an enriched experience for customers worldwide. This partnership exemplifies the essence of strategic alliances, where combined vision and resources forge a path to mutual prosperity and innovation.

In the dynamic landscape of global business, forming strategic partnerships emerges as a pivotal strategy for startups seeking to amplify their impact, diversify their capabilities, and penetrate new markets. This chapter delves into the nuanced art of alliance-building, exploring how the confluence of complementary strengths can unlock exponential growth and opportunities.

Why do partnerships matter? The answer lies in the manifold benefits they offer:

- **Resource Sharing:** Leveraging combined assets to achieve shared objectives.
- **Market Expansion:** Tapping into new demographics and geographies.
- **Innovation:** Pooling knowledge and expertise to drive breakthrough solutions.

Partnerships, akin to the joining of stars to form constellations, require careful navigation to ensure alignment in vision, culture, and goals. From joint ventures and technology collaborations to marketing alliances and vendor partnerships, we chart the course for identifying, negotiating, and cultivating relationships that not only align with but also elevate your startup's mission.

Opening Anecdote: Starbucks and Spotify – A Symphony of Success

When Starbucks and Spotify teamed up, it wasn't just about music or coffee. It was about enhancing the Starbucks experience through personalized playlists. This partnership reminds us that when two companies come together with a shared vision, the resulting synergy can be transformative.

The Partnership Paradigm: Two Heads are Better Than One

In a world of increasing competition, forming alliances can be the key to unlocking growth, accessing new markets, and fostering innovation.

Why Do Partnerships Matter?

• **Resource Sharing:** Combining skills, technology, and networks can lead to shared success.

• **Market Expansion:** Access new customers and regions, increasing brand visibility.

• **Innovation:** Collaborative efforts can produce groundbreaking solutions.

> *Quick Thought:*
> *Partnerships are like marriages. They require trust, mutual respect, and continuous effort to thrive.*

Types of Strategic Alliances:

1. **Joint Ventures:** Shared dreams, risks, and rewards.
2. **Distribution or Sales:** Expand without expanding; reach new customers through partners.
3. **Technology Collaboration:** Innovate through shared expertise.
4. **Marketing Alliances:** Double the noise, double the attention.
5. **Vendor Partnerships:** Strengthen the supply chain; optimize operations.

Scouting the Right Partners:

- **Compatibility Check:** It's not just about business. Do your values and cultures align?
- **Growth Alignment:** Will the partnership propel both parties forward?
- **Strength and Weakness Assessment:** Does the partnership fill gaps for both parties?

Case Study Deep Dive: GoPro & Red Bull – An Adrenaline-Fueled Partnership

Shared Audiences, Shared Thrills: At the heart of this partnership was a common demographic – adventure enthusiasts. GoPro, a brand synonymous with action-packed footage, and Red Bull, an energy drink associated with extreme sports, realized the potential of tapping into each other's fervent fanbase.

Complementary Branding: It wasn't just about slapping logos on each other's products. GoPro equipped athletes at Red Bull sponsored events with cameras, capturing exhilarating moments from unique perspectives. In return, Red Bull's events received massive exposure through GoPro's vast social media channels and distribution platforms.

Risk & Reward: By sharing sponsorship and marketing costs, both brands leveraged mutual benefits while mitigating individual risks. This symbiotic relationship ensured that one brand's success would ripple positively to the other.

Elevated Experiences: The partnership wasn't just transactional – it was transformative. Fans began associating the immersive first-person footage with the energy and exhilaration of a Red Bull experience, creating a unified brand message that resonated globally.

Case Study Deep Dive: Netflix & LG – Revolutionizing Entertainment Access

Expanding Horizons: As Netflix, a budding streaming service, sought to cement its position in the home entertainment segment, a strategic alliance was the key. LG, a global electronics giant, provided the perfect platform with its line of Smart TVs.

Seamless Integration: The partnership transcended a mere pre-installed app. It meant that every LG Smart TV owner was introduced to Netflix's world of content right from the setup process. This ease of access was a game-changer, lowering barriers to subscription and usage.

Mutual Benefits: For Netflix, the partnership exponentially expanded its user base and visibility. For LG, having a pre-installed Netflix app became a selling point, promoting their TVs as not just smart but "entertainment-ready".

The Future of Viewing: By predicting the shift from traditional cable TV to on-demand streaming, both Netflix and LG positioned themselves at the forefront of this change. Their alliance played a crucial role in molding viewer habits and expectations, setting new standards for the industry.

```
Pro Tip: Before formalizing any partnership, ensure a
trial run or pilot project. It helps in gauging the
partnership's practicality and potential.
```

Power in Partnerships

In the intricate dance of business, finding the right partner can lead your startup to new horizons. These alliances are about mutual growth, shared risks, and combined strengths. While not every partnership guarantees success, the right alliance can amplify your startup's capabilities and reach.

Exercise: Alliance-Building Workshop

Identifying and Analyzing Potential Partnerships:

1. **Partnership Mapping Exercise**: Begin by mapping out potential partners across various categories such as technology, distribution, marketing, and supply chain. For each potential partner, identify how they align with your startup's goals, values, and needs. Consider creating a matrix to evaluate these partnerships based on strategic importance and feasibility.

2. **Partnership Goal Setting**: For each identified potential partnership, articulate clear goals. What do you aim to achieve through this partnership? Goals could range from expanding your customer base, entering new markets, enhancing product offerings, or improving operational efficiencies. Ensure these goals are Specific, Measurable, Achievable, Relevant, and Time-bound (SMART).

3. **Value Proposition Crafting**: Develop a tailored value proposition for approaching potential partners. This should clearly outline what your startup brings to the table and how the partnership can create mutual value. Consider the unique assets, capabilities, or markets your startup can offer to a potential partner and how these align with their objectives.

Preparing for Partnership Engagement:

1. **Compatibility and Culture Assessment**: Conduct an in-depth analysis to assess the compatibility between your startup and each potential partner. This includes evaluating cultural alignment, business practices, and long-term strategic goals. Develop a checklist of key compatibility criteria to aid in this assessment.
2. **Strategic Alliance Blueprint**: Choose one potential partnership to focus on and create a detailed blueprint for this alliance. This blueprint should cover the structure of the partnership, key objectives, governance, how both parties will work together, and metrics for success. Include a plan for the initial pilot phase to test the partnership dynamics before a full-scale roll-out.
3. **Negotiation Strategy Plan**: Develop a negotiation strategy that includes your key terms and conditions, desired outcomes, and concessions you are willing to make. Prepare by understanding the potential partner's likely objectives and pressure points. Role-play different negotiation scenarios with a team member or advisor to refine your approach and tactics.

Reflecting and Moving Forward:

- **Partnership Reflection Journal**: After completing the exercises, maintain a journal to reflect on the insights gained and the potential impact of these strategic partnerships on your startup's trajectory. Note any apprehensions, the anticipated challenges in forming and maintaining these alliances, and how they can be addressed.

- **Actionable Partnership Engagement Plan**: Based on your analyses and preparation, outline an actionable plan for engaging with the identified potential partners. Set timelines for initial outreach, meetings, and evaluations. This plan should also include strategies for maintaining and growing the partnership over time, with regular check-ins and feedback loops to ensure alignment and adapt to any changes.

Challenge For You:

Design a partnership proposal for a company you admire. Focus on the mutual benefits and shared vision.

Coming Up Next:

A deep dive into the continuous evolution of startups. In a rapidly changing world, adaptability is not just a choice but a necessity. How can your startup maintain agility, embrace change, and turn challenges into opportunities? Join us on this insightful journey.

9

Staying Ahead: Continuous Learning and Adaptation

"It is not the strongest of the species that survives, nor the most intelligent;
it is the one most responsive to change."
— Charles Darwin

As we navigate further into the uncharted territories of entrepreneurship, "Staying Ahead: Continuous Learning and Adaptation" emerges as the beacon that guides us through the evolving landscape of business. In the tale of Kodak's moment of realization, we are reminded of the critical importance of foresight and flexibility. This narrative is not merely about the missed opportunities of a bygone era but a clarion call to embrace the ethos of perpetual growth and adaptability in our ventures.

In the realm of startups, where the winds of change are both swift and unpredictable, the capacity for continuous learning and the agility to adapt are not merely advantageous—they are essential for survival. This chapter is dedicated to unraveling the art and science of staying relevant in a world that never ceases to evolve. It's an odyssey into transforming learning into a relentless quest for knowledge and turning adaptation into a strategic advantage.

Why is continuous learning the cornerstone of enduring success? It's the engine that propels startups beyond the competition, through the refinement of products and services, and towards the forefront of innovation. It cultivates a culture that thrives on curiosity, resilience, and the pursuit of excellence.

As we dissect the anatomy of adaptation, we explore how the dynamic interplay between learning and applying new insights can sculpt a startup's path through fluctuating markets, emerging disruptions, and the ever-expanding horizon of opportunities. This journey through the landscape of continuous learning and adaptation equips you with the strategies to not only anticipate change but to harness it, crafting a future where your startup not only survives but thrives.

Opening Anecdote: The Kodak Moment of Realization

In the 1970s, Kodak, the photographic giant, had the technology to develop digital photography. However, they clung to their film-based business model. By the time they realized the potential of digital, the world had moved on. Kodak's story emphasizes the dire need for continuous learning and quick adaptation in business.

Learning: An Ongoing Quest, Not a Destination

Continuous learning isn't about occasional updates. It's the relentless pursuit of betterment, new methodologies, and the latest industry advancements.

Reasons to Embrace Continuous Learning:

- **Survival in the Competitive Landscape:** With evolving technology and emerging competitors, learning keeps your startup relevant.
- **Refinement & Enhancement:** Using customer feedback and industry trends to improve products/services.
- **Innovation's Backbone:** Continuous learning breeds groundbreaking ideas.
- **The Heartbeat of a Thriving Culture:** Encouraging a learning environment leads to a motivated, inquisitive, and dynamic team.

Quick Thought:
Just like a shark needs to keep moving to stay alive, startups need to keep learning to thrive.

The Essence of Adaptation in the Startup Universe
Adaptation is the actionable counterpart of learning. It's about integrating newfound knowledge into practical business strategies.

Entrepreneurship in Action: Key Ingredients

- **Fluctuating Markets:** Keeping up with changing consumer needs and industry trends.
- **Dancing with Disruptions:** Preemptively navigating

through unpredictable challenges.

- **The Path to Proliferation:** Exploring new avenues and adapting to scale and expand.

Continuous Learning & Adaptation in Action: Turning Knowledge to Power

- **Promotion of Open Dialogue:** Encourage a feedback-rich environment. Insights are the building blocks of innovation.
- **Maintain Curiosity:** Regularly engage in new learning opportunities, from seminars to online courses.
- **The Test & Tweak Approach:** Pilot new ideas, measure outcomes, learn, and refine. Embrace the cycle of improvement.
- **Building Resilience:** Prepare to switch gears when needed. Stay agile and view challenges as growth catalysts.

Case Study Deep Dive: Nokia – The Rise, Fall, and Return to Relevance

Dominance to Decline: Once the undisputed king of the mobile phone market, Nokia's handsets were synonymous with reliability and innovation in the 1990s and early 2000s. But the advent of smartphones, led by Apple's iPhone and Android OS, disrupted Nokia's comfortable market position.

Failure to Adapt: Nokia's Symbian OS was quickly overshadowed by more user-friendly interfaces from competitors. Despite realizing the threat, Nokia's response was slow and lackluster. When they finally chose to pivot, they committed to Microsoft's Windows Phone OS, which was also struggling against Android and iOS.

Learning and Rebirth: After selling its phone division to Microsoft in 2014, Nokia could have faded into history. But instead, they focused on reinventing themselves, diving deep into the network infrastructure business and returning to the mobile world with a series of Android-powered handsets. Their recent ventures highlight a rejuvenated focus on learning from past mistakes and adapting to the current market landscape.

Resilience and Reinvention: Today, while Nokia might not command the same dominance in handsets, they remain a powerful testament to the importance of continuous learning, adaptability, and the courage to reinvent oneself amidst market upheavals.

Case Study Deep Dive: BlackBerry – From Smartphone Kingpin to Security Software Specialist

The Peak of Prowess: At the height of its success in the late 2000s, BlackBerry (then known as Research In Motion or RIM) was a symbol of corporate success. Business professionals worldwide were drawn to its efficient email service, secure platform, and physical keyboard. Its devices, often referred to as "CrackBerries" due to their addictive nature, dominated the corporate world.

The Onset of Obsolescence: BlackBerry's golden period began to wane with the advent of touchscreen smartphones. Apple's iPhone and a slew of Android devices started to redefine what a smartphone should offer: a broad range of apps, high-quality cameras, and an intuitive touchscreen interface. BlackBerry underestimated this shift, holding on to its belief that its core clientele, the business professionals, would remain loyal.

Missed Signals: While BlackBerry did recognize the changing winds and released its touchscreen phone, the BlackBerry Storm, in 2008, the device was riddled with issues. Their delayed response to the App economy and the appeal of the iOS App Store and Google Play Store meant that they lost many of their users to platforms that offered a richer ecosystem.

The Road to Reinvention: Recognizing the decline in their handset market share, BlackBerry made a bold decision. They shifted their primary focus from handsets to enterprise software and services, leveraging their reputation for security. This move has seen them establish themselves in fields like car software and cybersecurity.

Embracing Adaptation: BlackBerry's story is one of highs, lows, and reinvention. While they might not be the smartphone giants they once were, their pivot into software and security showcases their ability to learn and adapt in the face of adversity. It serves as a poignant reminder that continuous learning and swift adaptation are key to navigating the tumultuous waters of the tech industry.

```
Pro Tip: Foster a culture where 'not knowing' is okay
but not 'learning' is not. It's okay to make
mistakes; it's not okay to repeat them without
learning.
```

The Dynamic Dance of Learning and Adaptation

A startup that continually learns and adapts is like a river: always flowing, reshaping, and carving its path. Remember Kodak's missed opportunities or Netflix's proactive adaptations? The line between stagnation and success is drawn by learning and adaptation.

Exercise: Cultivating Continuous Learning and Adaptation

Building a Learning Ecosystem:

1. **Learning Agenda Creation**: Identify key areas where you and your team need to deepen your knowledge to stay competitive. This could include emerging technologies, market trends, or operational excellence. Set up a learning calendar that allocates time for team learning sessions, webinars, and workshops.
2. **Knowledge Sharing Platform**: Develop a platform or system within your startup for sharing insights, articles, and resources discovered by team members. This could be a digital bulletin board, a weekly newsletter, or a dedicated time during team meetings for sharing key learnings.
3. **Adaptation Workshop**: Conduct a workshop with your team to analyze recent industry changes or case studies of companies that failed to adapt. Use these discussions to draw lessons on how your startup can remain agile and responsive to change.

Implementing Adaptation Strategies:

1. **Feedback Integration Process**: Establish a structured process for collecting feedback from customers, employees, and partners. This process should include mecha-

nisms for evaluating feedback, deciding on actions, and implementing changes. Make this an integral part of your product development and customer service strategies.

2. **Scenario Planning Exercise**: Engage your team in scenario planning exercises that explore potential future changes in your industry, such as new technologies, regulations, or consumer behaviors. Develop strategies for how your startup would respond to these scenarios, focusing on flexibility and innovation.

3. **Innovation Challenges**: Regularly organize innovation challenges that encourage your team to think creatively about new products, services, or processes. Provide a theme or problem to solve, and allocate resources for prototyping the most promising ideas. This fosters a culture of innovation and adaptability.

Reflecting on Growth and Change:

- **Adaptation Diary**: Keep an adaptation diary where you document the changes your startup has made in response to new learnings or feedback. Reflect on the impact of these adaptations on your business operations, team dynamics, and customer satisfaction.
- **Continuous Improvement Meetings**: Schedule monthly continuous improvement meetings where your team reviews what has been learned and how the startup has adapted. Use these meetings to celebrate successes, learn from mistakes, and plan future learning and adaptation initiatives.

Challenge For You:

This month, identify one major learning point and see how you can practically adapt it into your startup's operations.

Coming Up Next:

The next chapter delves into the maze of exit strategies and acquisitions. As the entrepreneurial journey approaches its next significant phase, understanding these pathways becomes paramount. Join us as we light the way.

10

The Art of Exit: Strategies and Acquisitions

"In the end, all business operations can be reduced to three words:
people, product, and profits."
— Lee Iacocca

Venturing deeper into the heart of entrepreneurial mastery, "The Art of Exit: Strategies and Acquisitions" unfolds as a pivotal exploration into the strategic finales and transitions that crown the lifecycle of startups. The Instagram story, a golden exit par excellence, serves as a compelling prelude to this narrative, underscoring the significance of foresight, timing, and the audacious vision that can transform a nascent startup into a global phenomenon. This tale is not merely about the financial windfall; it's a testament to the strategic acumen that discerns the untapped potential lying beyond the present.

Exiting, in the entrepreneurial odyssey, is a multifaceted maneuver that encompasses more than the pursuit of profit. It's the culmination of relentless passion, innovation, and the journey towards building something of enduring value. This chapter delves into the art and science of crafting exit strategies that resonate with the core ethos of your venture, ensuring that the transition not only rewards financially but also aligns with the broader vision and legacy of your startup.

As we chart the course through the myriad exit pathways—from the allure of acquisitions and the grandeur of IPOs to the strategic foresight behind mergers and management buyouts—we illuminate the preparations, negotiations, and considerations pivotal to navigating these waters. This exploration is not just about charting exits; it's about understanding how these strategic decisions can amplify the impact, reach, and essence of what you've built.

Opening Anecdote: The Instagram Golden Exit

In 2012, a rapidly blossoming photo-sharing app named Instagram caught the attention of social media titan, Facebook. Despite Instagram not having a revenue model in place, Mark Zuckerberg made a strategic decision to acquire it for a staggering $1 billion. Why? He perceived the immense potential it held. Today, Instagram stands as one of the most potent social media platforms. This story emphasizes the importance of timing and vision in the exit landscape.

Demystifying Exit Strategies: Beyond Just Profit

Every entrepreneur's journey is marked by milestones, and for many, a successful exit is a crowning glory. But it's more than just a financial transaction; it's the culmination of years of passion, hard work, and resilience. Let's explore the different avenues through which startups can transition or evolve:

1. **Acquisition**: The Instagram Tale
   The allure of acquisition lies not just in the monetary aspect but also in the potential to amplify the product's reach, as evidenced by Instagram's integration into Facebook's ecosystem.
2. **Initial Public Offering (IPO)**: Alibaba's Grand Debut
   When Jack Ma founded Alibaba, it was a small startup in Hangzhou. Its 2014 IPO, which garnered a record-breaking $25 billion, underscored the transformative power of belief and vision.
3. **Management Buyout (MBO)**: Steering the Ship - The Asda Chronicles
   When Asda's leadership decided to take charge and acquire the company, it showcased an intense commitment to the brand's vision and future.
4. **Merger**: Coming Together for Greater Might - Exxon Mobil's Confluence
   When Exxon and Mobil decided to merge, it wasn't just about pooling resources; it was about creating an energy behemoth that could redefine industry standards.

Preparation: Setting the Stage for a Graceful Exit

Just as a dancer rehearses before the final performance, entrepreneurs must meticulously prepare for their exit. This involves:

- **Solidifying the Foundation**: Aim for steady growth and profitability. This not only increases your venture's appeal but also stands as a testament to its potential.
- **Documentation**: Remember, clarity breeds confidence. Ensure all financial and operational records are systematic,

transparent, and easily accessible.

- **Protect Your Crown Jewels**: Any intellectual property, be it patents, trademarks, or copyrights, can drastically elevate your company's valuation. Safeguard them with rigor.

At The Negotiating Table: Crafting a Win-Win

As with any significant decision, an exit involves intricate negotiations. It's a dance of numbers, visions, and aspirations. Seek guidance from experts, be it M&A advisors, legal consultants, or financial wizards. Their experience can help streamline the process and optimize outcomes.

> ### Quick Thought:
> *Your startup is your legacy. An exit strategy isn't about ending this legacy, but about giving it a new direction, a broader horizon.*

Case Study: Rent the Runway – A Fashion Revolution

The Genesis: In 2009, Jennifer Hyman and Jennifer Fleiss launched Rent the Runway, a platform that would change the dynamics of luxury fashion by allowing women to rent designer apparel and accessories. The idea was revolutionary: why buy a designer dress you'd wear once when you could rent it for a fraction of the cost?

Scaling Up: With a growing subscriber base and expanding inventory, Rent the Runway quickly caught the eye of investors. Their unique model of the "closet in the cloud" was not only sustainable but also resonated with the modern consumer's mindset.

The Path Not Taken (Yet): While many anticipated Rent the Runway to go public, especially after reaching 'unicorn' status with a valuation over $1 billion, the company has thus far chosen to remain private. Their focus remains on growing their subscriber base, expanding offerings, and driving sustainability in the fashion industry.

Lessons: Rent the Runway demonstrates that an exit isn't the only measure of success. Sometimes, retaining control and focusing on growth and vision can be equally, if not more, rewarding.

Case Study: Sundial Brands – From Harlem to Global Impact

Rooted Beginnings: Sundial Brands, the parent company of SheaMoisture, was founded in 1991 by Liberian immigrants, including Richelieu Dennis. The brand, rooted in African and African American heritage, offered products catering to the specific needs of Black hair and skin.

Bridging the Gap: SheaMoisture aimed to fill a glaring void in the beauty market, addressing the unique hair and skincare needs of Black women, a segment that was largely overlooked by major beauty brands.

The Unilever Acquisition: Recognizing the brand's potential and its dedicated customer base, global conglomerate Unilever acquired Sundial Brands in 2017. But this wasn't just any acquisition. Unilever and Sundial Brands also pledged $50 million to empower women of color entrepreneurs.

Growth and Legacy: Post-acquisition, Sundial Brands

retained its identity and continued its mission. Richelieu Dennis used the proceeds from the sale to launch the New Voices Fund to support Black women entrepreneurs and even bought Madam C.J. Walker's estate to transform it into an incubator for Black women in business.

Key Takeaway: Sundial Brands showcases how an acquisition can be more than a business transaction—it can be a platform for greater social impact and legacy.

```
Pro Tip: Always approach an exit with clarity and not
haste. Remember, it's about maximizing value, not
just in terms of money but also in terms of potential
and legacy.
```

Concluding Thoughts: A New Dawn, Not The End

An exit isn't the conclusion of your entrepreneurial tale; it's a new chapter. Whether it's watching your brand soar to new heights post-acquisition or seeing it make waves on the stock exchange, the journey continues.

Exercise: Navigating Your Exit Strategy

Planning for Your Exit:

1. **Exit Strategy Brainstorming**: Gather your leadership team for a brainstorming session to discuss potential exit strategies. Consider the pros and cons of each method (e.g., acquisition, IPO, MBO) in the context of your startup's current position and future aspirations. Document these discussions to refer back to as your company evolves.

2. **Legacy and Impact Visualization**: Reflect deeply on the legacy you want to leave through your startup. Create a vision board or write a detailed narrative that encapsulates the impact and legacy you envision. How does each potential exit strategy align with or detract from this vision?

3. **Financial Preparedness Workshop**: Conduct a workshop focused on understanding the financial implications of various exit strategies. Involve your finance team or external advisors to analyze your startup's valuation, potential market conditions, and financial readiness for exit scenarios.

Preparing for Transition:

1. **Succession Planning**: Regardless of the exit strategy you lean towards, succession planning is crucial. Outline a plan that ensures the continuity of leadership and the preservation of the company culture. Identify potential leaders within your organization who could steer the company post-exit.

2. **Intellectual Property Audit**: Conduct a thorough audit of your startup's intellectual property (IP) assets. Understanding the full scope and value of your IP can significantly impact your exit strategy and valuation. Consider consulting with an IP attorney to ensure all assets are properly protected and leveraged in exit negotiations.

3. **Acquirer Research Assignment**: Assign your team the task of researching potential acquirers or partners. Look for companies that have a strategic interest in your startup's market, technology, or team. Develop a dossier

on each, noting how a partnership or acquisition could offer mutual benefits.

Reflecting and Preparing for Dialogue:

- **Stakeholder Analysis**: Identify and analyze key stakeholders who will be affected by your exit strategy, including employees, investors, customers, and partners. Plan how to address their concerns and how they will be informed and involved in the transition process.
- **Negotiation Role-Play**: Engage in role-play exercises to prepare for exit negotiations. This should include various scenarios, such as negotiating with potential acquirers or discussing terms with investors for an IPO. Focus on honing your communication skills, understanding the other party's perspective, and finding common ground.

Challenge For You:

Reflect on your exit strategy this month. How does it align with your startup's long-term vision and the legacy you wish to leave behind?

Coming Up Next:

As we wrap up this guide, we'll connect all the dots, emphasizing the holistic nature of the entrepreneurial journey. Ready to culminate this adventure with key takeaways and forward momentum? Let's delve in.

11

The Entrepreneurial Expedition: Charting Your Course

Embarking on an entrepreneurial venture is not just about creating a business; it's a testament to the continuous journey of discovery, resilience, and innovation. From the inception of an idea to its final realization, this path is strewn with both challenges and triumphs. The spirit to persevere, combined with the wisdom acquired from each experience, shapes a successful entrepreneur.

This guide has led you through every critical phase of a startup's lifecycle. As we round off, let's summarize the key lessons and extend additional resources for your ongoing voyage.

9 Key Takeaways

1. **Ideation and Validation:** The journey commences with an idea. Its success lies in understanding the market demand, competition, and ensuring it addresses a genuine need.

2. **Building a Foundational Framework:** A robust business plan, coupled with clarity on your target audience, value proposition, and business model, lays the groundwork for future success.

3. **The MVP Phase:** This stage allows for real-time testing. It emphasizes the importance of user feedback, iterative development, and delivering core value.

4. **Launch and Early Growth:** Effective marketing strategies, understanding your target audience, and consistently tracking progress ensures steady growth in the initial stages.

5. **Scaling and Operations:** As the business expands, focusing on scalability, efficient processes, and a strong organizational culture becomes imperative.

6. **Funding and Financing:** A successful pitch, comprehensive understanding of financials, and showcasing growth potential are crucial for securing investments.

7. **Strategic Partnerships:** Collaborative efforts can amplify growth. Identify partners whose goals align with yours to unlock new possibilities.

8. **Continuous Learning and Adaptation:** The business landscape is dynamic. Staying receptive to feedback, fostering innovation, and remaining agile ensures long-term success.

9. **Exit Strategies:** Planning an exit is as essential as the launch. Understand various exit avenues and align them with your business goals for a successful culmination.

Resources for Continued Growth

Online Tools & Platforms

1. **Lean Canvas Tool** - Quickly sketch out your startup's business model. URL: www.leancanvas.com
2. **Persona Generator (HubSpot)** - Create detailed buyer personas for target audience identification. URL: www.hubspot.com/make-my-persona
3. **Crunchbase** - Essential for researching investors, competitors, and industry trends. A valuable resource for startups looking to understand their market position and potential investment opportunities. URL: www.crunchbase.com
4. **Trello** - An intuitive project management tool that helps in organizing tasks, tracking progress, and facilitating team collaboration. Perfect for managing and visualizing project workflows. URL: www.trello.com
5. **Mailchimp** - Offers marketing automation and email marketing services, ideal for startups looking to build and engage their customer base through newsletters and targeted campaigns. URL: www.mailchimp.com
6. **Canva** - A user-friendly graphic design tool that allows startups to create professional-quality visual content, from social media graphics to presentations, without needing extensive design skills. URL: www.canva.com
7. **SurveyMonkey** - Provides online survey tools, making it easier for startups to gather customer feedback, conduct market research, and test new ideas quickly. URL: www.surveymonkey.com

Books & Publications

1. **"Value Proposition Design" by Alexander Oster-walder** - Guide to creating compelling value propositions. URL: www.strategyzer.com/books/value-proposition-design
2. **"Business Model Generation" by Alexander Oster-walder and Yves Pigneur** - Comprehensive guide on various business models. URL: www.strategyzer.com/books/business-model-generation
3. **"The Lean Startup" by Eric Ries** - A seminal book that introduces the lean startup methodology, emphasizing the importance of agile development, MVPs, and iterative design to startup success. URL: www.theleanstartup.com
4. **"Zero to One" by Peter Thiel with Blake Masters** - Offers unconventional wisdom on startup innovation, competition, and building a successful venture that goes from 0 to 1 rather than from 1 to n. URL: www.zerotoonebook.com
5. **"Hooked: How to Build Habit-Forming Products" by Nir Eyal** - Explores the psychology behind what makes products addictive and provides insights on how startups can create products that capture user attention. URL: www.nirandfar.com/hooked
6. **"Crossing the Chasm" by Geoffrey A. Moore** - Focuses on the challenges startups face when transitioning from early adopters to the mainstream market and strategies to successfully make this leap. URL: www.geoffreyamoore.com/books/crossing-the-chasm

Podcasts & Video Channels

1. **How I Built This with Guy Raz** - A podcast that delves into the stories behind some of the world's best-known companies and the entrepreneurs who built them from the ground up. URL: NPR's How I Built This
2. **Y Combinator's YouTube Channel** - Offers a wealth of startup-related content, including talks from industry leaders, advice on pitching and fundraising, and insights on growing your business. URL: Y Combinator YouTube Channel

The entrepreneurial path is a unique blend of challenges and celebrations. The learning never ceases, and adaptability is the key. Let this guide be a cornerstone, but remember to forge your own path, draw insights from your experiences, and always be ready to learn. The entrepreneurial world awaits your mark. Best wishes on your continued journey!

Epilogue: Lighting the Beacon for Future Entrepreneurs

As the final words of "Unicorn Manifesto: The Ascent of an Entrepreneur from Startup to Acquisition" resonate in the quiet aftermath of your journey through its pages, I invite you to pause and reflect on the odyssey you've just embarked upon. This isn't merely the end of a book; it's the dawn of your entrepreneurial voyage—a journey that promises to be as challenging as it is rewarding, as daunting as it is exhilarating.

Twenty years ago, inspired by the pioneering insights of Timothy Ferriss's "The 4-Hour Workweek," I embarked on my own entrepreneurial quest. Ferriss's work ignited a flame within me, a desire to redefine what it means to be an entrepreneur in an evolving business landscape. Today, as I share the culmination of two decades of experience, challenges, and triumphs through this series, my hope is that "Unicorn Manifesto" serves as your Ferriss moment—a spark that ignites your passion, determination, and unyielding drive to succeed.

Remember, the path of entrepreneurship is as diverse as the individuals who walk it. Your journey will be unique, marked by its highs and lows, successes and setbacks. But it's in navigating these experiences that true growth occurs. This book, and the series it introduces, is designed to be your compass, guiding you through the complexities of entrepreneurship, from the seed of an idea to the pinnacle of acquisition.

"Unicorn Manifesto" is more than a guide; it's a call to action— to build businesses that not only thrive but also contribute positively to society and the environment. As we close this chapter and you stand on the threshold of your adventure, remember that being an entrepreneur is about more than creating a successful business. It's about becoming a beacon of innovation, leadership, and impact.

As you move forward, carry with you the lessons, insights, and inspirations from these pages. Let them fuel your journey, inspire your decisions, and remind you that in the world of entrepreneurship, there are no limits to what you can achieve. The only boundaries are those you set for yourself.

So, dear reader, as you close this book, don't see it as an end but as a beginning—the first step on your path to becoming a unicorn in your own right. The world awaits your ideas, your passion, and your contribution. Embrace the journey with an open heart and an unwavering spirit.

And remember, in the vast universe of entrepreneurship, you are not alone. We are all part of a continuum—a legacy of innovators, dreamers, and builders who have dared to believe that they can make a difference. As you forge your path, know that you are adding your chapter to a much larger story—one of courage, innovation, and purpose.

Onward to your ascent, where dreams take flight, and the impossible becomes your reality.

The Ask

Dear Esteemed Entrepreneur,

Has our shared voyage ignited the spark of a unicorn within your spirit? Should "Unicorn Manifesto" have cast a light on your path towards entrepreneurial greatness, might I invite you to share your wisdom through a review on Amazon? Whether you find this work to be a beacon of inspiration or have valuable feedback to enhance its journey, each perspective is a treasure as we aim to embolden future generations of unicorns.

Craving further exploration? Visit my Amazon author page (https://www.amazon.com/author/patrickhperrine) to deepen your entrepreneurial understanding. Together, let's champion the entrepreneurial spirit, one heartfelt review at a time.

With Sincere Appreciation,
    Patrick

About the Author

Patrick H. Perrine is a trailblazing author, mentor, and seasoned entrepreneur with a spirit that exemplifies the essence of entrepreneurship. From his humble beginnings as a paperboy in Minnesota to his emergence as a globally recognized industry leader, his journey epitomizes resilience and determination.

Fueled by an insatiable thirst for knowledge, Patrick opted for university over his senior high school year, setting the stage for his relentless pursuit of personal growth. His tenure with UpStart, an organization championing educational opportunities for first-generation Americans, ignited his lifelong commitment to empowering others, extending beyond business and into his early philanthropic endeavors.

In his twenties, Patrick served as a Founding Board member for The Point Foundation, the largest LGBTQ scholarship foundation today. His dedication to fostering inclusivity and aiding LGBTQ students in higher education continues to positively impact hundreds of lives.

Patrick's entrepreneurial journey took flight with myPartner.com, an online dating service that addressed a critical gap in the market. Recognized as one of the "Best Matchmakers" and "Most Innovative Online Dating Sites" by the iDate Industry, the venture earned a Certificate of Recognition issued by California Legislature Assemblyman Mark Leno. This marked Patrick's first step in a journey filled with identifying unique opportunities and delivering transformative solutions across industries from skincare to dog tech.

Despite the hurdles encountered, Patrick's determination only amplified. His passion for nurturing startups led him to establish Rincon Hill Advisors. During this period, he served as a Steering Committee member for StartOut, a leading nonprofit fostering queer entrepreneurship, and consulted with Fortune 500 companies like Berkshire Hathaway and Intuit.

Adding to his achievements as an entrepreneur, Patrick became an angel investor. His foresight led him to invest in promising startups like MisterB&B, the world's largest gay hotelier, and Roadster, the leading commerce platform for car buying. His dog tech venture, too, gained recognition, leading to his selection as a NGLCC Pitch Finalist and participant in the Seamless IoT Accelerator, earning a $100,000 investment offer as a program graduate.

Most recently, Patrick served as an Entrepreneur in Residence (EiR) with 500 StartUps, an organization committed to uplifting global economies through entrepreneurship. This role solidified his dedication to guiding and uplifting aspiring entrepreneurs.

With multiple books to his credit, including recent works "Fail Fast, Recover Faster", "Ignite Your Dream", and "Fueling the Fire," Patrick continues to share his journey and insights. His writing reflects his unwavering commitment to guiding entrepreneurs through their unique journeys.

Patrick H. Perrine is more than a summary of his accomplishments. He stands as a testament to the power of determination, innovation, and a generous spirit. His contributions have been acknowledged in global press publications such as Forbes, Advocate, and Mirror, but his most profound impact lies in the lives of the entrepreneurs he's guided, inspired, and empowered. As he continues sharing his wisdom in the 10 volume series "Be A Unicorn: The New Entrepreneur's Ultimate Guide to Success," Patrick personifies the quintessential entrepreneurial journey—one of resilience, innovation, and the relentless pursuit of personal growth.

Subscribe to my newsletter:

✉ https://patrickperrine.com

Also by Patrick H. Perrine

Your next adventure in entrepreneurship awaits! Choose your guidebook on Amazon (https://www.amazon.com/author/patrickhperrine) or **www.PatrickPerrine.com**, and ignite the spark that takes your venture to new heights. The future is yours to shape!

Unicorn Rising: Ascending to the Pinnacle of Entrepreneurship and the Billionaire's Club
Fueled by entrepreneurial dreams and the allure of the Unicorn Club? Patrick H. Perrine is your guide, offering an unparalleled roadmap set to be every entrepreneur's playbook.

"Unicorn Rising" emerges as the cornerstone of the *Be A Unicorn* series, laying the groundwork that "Unicorn Manifesto" and the other nine volumes build upon.

This seminal work provides an in-depth exploration into the entrepreneurial journey, offering a comprehensive roadmap for those aiming to scale their ventures to the heights of the Unicorn Club.

Driven by the dream of entrepreneurial excellence and a place in the Unicorn Club? Patrick H. Perrine offers an unmatched guide, positioning this book as the ultimate playbook for entrepreneurs.

Within "Unicorn Rising," readers will find a guide not just to achieving lofty valuations, but to navigating the realms of innovation, transformative leadership, and enduring success. It offers insights into the nuances of leadership, the forefront of emerging technologies, financial mastery, and the core of impactful entrepreneurship.

This series acknowledges the uniqueness of each entrepreneurial journey. Patrick delivers foundational wisdom alongside practical tools, emphasizing the tailored path each startup must navigate. Whether you're just beginning your entrepreneurial quest or are a seasoned professional fine-tuning your strategy, this book, and its series, light the way.

Step forward, challenge the status quo, and with "Unicorn Rising," ascend to unprecedented heights in your entrepreneurial venture.

Ignite Your Dream: The Quintessential Checklist for Aspiring Entrepreneurs
Ignite Your Dream: The Quintessential Checklist for Aspiring Entrepreneurs" by Patrick H. Perrine is an immersive guide lighting the path towards entrepreneurial success.

This power-packed handbook propels you from dreaming to achieving with a carefully curated 100-step map. Dive into real-life entrepreneur stories, extract wisdom, and utilize actionable checklists. This book transcends theoretical guidelines, providing a mentorship experience designed to turn dreams into reality.

Ready to kindle your entrepreneurial spirit? "Ignite your Dream" is your step forward towards unlocking potential and achieving success in the exciting world of entrepreneurship.

Fail Fast, Recover Faster: Bouncing Back From Entrepreneurial Failure

Embrace failure and bounce back stronger with "Fail Fast, Recover Faster: Bouncing Back From Entrepreneurial Failure". It's your guidebook through the tumultuous journey of entrepreneurship, celebrating stumbles as stepping stones towards success.

Dive into compelling tales of triumphant entrepreneurs, learn how to pivot rapidly, manage fallout, and convert setbacks into launchpads. Discover strategies for repairing financial, relationship, and reputation damage, and see your failures as badges of resilience.

This transformative book readies you to rebound from failure swiftly, turning your setbacks into your next entrepreneurial triumph. With "Fail Fast, Recover Faster", you're poised to harness your own unicorn moment and turn failure into a launching pad for success.

Fueling the Fire: Nurturing Resilience and Preventing Burnout in Entrepreneurship

In "Fueling the Fire: Nurturing Resilience and Preventing Burnout in Entrepreneurship," seasoned entrepreneur Patrick H. Perrine guides you through the entrepreneurial journey, sharing practical strategies for maintaining resilience and passion.

Drawing from 20 years of startup experience, Perrine covers everything from ideation to acquisition. Discover how to build a support system, manage your time effectively, cultivate a positive work culture, and align your work with your values.

Whether you're an experienced entrepreneur or just beginning, "Fueling the Fire" is a must-read for maintaining balance and fulfillment in the dynamic world of entrepreneurship.